N. T.
FOR
BIBLE STUDY GUIDES

GALATIANS

10 STUDIES FOR INDIVIDUALS OR GROUPS

N. T. WRIGHT

WITH DALE & SANDY LARSEN

IVP Connect
An imprint of InterVarsity Press
Downers Grove, Illinois

InterVarsity Press
P.O. Box 1400, Downers Grove, IL 60515-1426
World Wide Web: www.ivpress.com
E-mail: email@ivpress.com

This study guide is based on and includes excerpts adapted from Paul for Everyone: Galatians and
Thessalonians, ©2002, Nicholas Thomas Wright. All Scripture quotations, unless otherwise indicated,
are taken from the New Testament for Everyone. Copyright ©2002-2008 by Nicholas Thomas Wright.
Used by permission of SPCK, London. All rights reserved.

InterVarsity Press® is the book-publishing division of InterVarsity Christian Fellowship/USA®, a student
movement active on campus at hundreds of universities, colleges and schools of nursing in the United
States of America, and a member movement of the International Fellowship of Evangelical Students.
For information about local and regional activities, write Public Relations Dept., InterVarsity Christian
Fellowship/USA, 6400 Schroeder Rd., P.O. Box 7895, Madison, WI 53707-7895, or visit the IVCF website
at <www.intervarsity.org>.

Cover design: Cindy Kiple
Cover image: Jean Pierre Pieuchot/Getty Images

ISBN 978-0-8308-2189-1

Printed in the United States of America ∞

InterVarsity Press is committed to protecting the environment and to the responsible use of
natural resources. As a member of Green Press Initiative we use recycled paper whenever
possible. To learn more about the Green Press Initiative, visit <www.greenpressinitiative.org>.

P	18	17	16	15	14	13	12	11	10	9	8	7	6	5	4	3	2	1
Y	25	24	23	22	21	20	19	18	17	16	15	14	13	12	11	10		

CONTENTS

GETTING THE MOST OUT OF GALATIANS

Imagine you're in South Africa in the 1970s. Apartheid is at its height. You are embarked on a risky project: to build a community center where everybody will be equally welcome, no matter what their color or race. You've designed it; you've laid the foundation in such a way that only the right sort of building can be built. Or so you think.

You are called away urgently to another part of the country. A little later you get a letter. A new group of builders are building on your foundation. They have changed the design, and are installing two meeting rooms, with two front doors, one for whites only and one for blacks only. Some of the local people are mightily relieved. They always thought there was going to be trouble, putting everyone together like that. Others, though, asked the builders why the original idea wouldn't do. Oh, said the builders airily, that chap who laid the foundation, he had some funny ideas. He didn't really have permission to make that design. He'd got a bit muddled. We're from the real authorities. This is how it's got to be.

That was the sort of situation in which Paul found himself, almost two thousand years ago in what is now south central Turkey. He was building with people, not bricks and mortar, laying the foundation of the good news. The one creator God had unveiled his long-awaited plan for the world in his son Jesus who was executed by the Romans but raised by God. The good news doesn't end there either. Jesus' death and resurrection mean that God is now building a new family, a single family, a family with no divisions, no separate races, no Jews at this table and Gentiles at another.

Afterward others came in saying Paul didn't really know what he was doing. He didn't have proper authority from the apostles in Jerusalem. Yes, we all believe that Jesus is the Messiah, they said; but we can't have Jewish believers and Gentile believers living as though they were part of the same family. If the Gentile believers want to be part of the real inner circle, they have to become Jews first.

Paul was so incensed that he wrote a sharp letter to the Galatians—one of the first, perhaps the very first, that Paul ever wrote to one of the young churches he planted on the eastern rim of the Mediterranean. (For more on this letter also see my *Paul for Everyone: Galatians and Thessalonians,* published by SPCK and Westminster John Knox, on which this guide is based.) That means it is among the very earliest documents we possess from the beginning of the church's existence.

Through this guide, prepared with the help of Dale and Sandy Larsen for which I am grateful, we will see a group of people already full of life, bubbling with energy, with questions, problems, excitement, danger and, above all, a sense of the presence and power of the living God who has changed the world through Jesus and is now at work in a new way by his Spirit. We all look for those same qualities to touch us as well as we delve more deeply into them.

SUGGESTIONS FOR INDIVIDUAL STUDY

1. As you begin each study, pray that God will speak to you through his Word.

2. Read the introduction to the study and respond to the "Open" question that follows it. This is designed to help you get into the theme of the study.

3. Read and reread the Bible passage to be studied. Each study is designed to help you consider the meaning of the passage in its context. The commentary and questions in this guide are based on my own translation of each passage found in the companion volume to

this guide in the For Everyone series on the New Testament (published by SPCK and Westminster John Knox).

4. Write your answers to the questions in the spaces provided or in a personal journal. Each study includes three types of questions: observation questions, which ask about the basic facts in the passage; interpretation questions, which delve into the meaning of the passage; and application questions, which help you discover the implications of the text for growing in Christ. Writing out your responses can bring clarity and deeper understanding of yourself and of God's Word.

5. Each session features selected comments from the For Everyone series. These notes provide further biblical and cultural background and contextual information. They are designed not to answer the questions for you but to help you along as you study the Bible for yourself. For even more reflections on each passage, you may wish to have on hand a copy of the companion volume from the For Everyone series as you work through this study guide.

6. Use the guidelines in the "Pray" section to focus on God, thanking him for what you have learned and praying about the applications that have come to mind.

SUGGESTIONS FOR GROUP MEMBERS

1. Come to the study prepared. Follow the suggestions for individual study mentioned above. You will find that careful preparation will greatly enrich your time spent in group discussion.

2. Be willing to participate in the discussion. The leader of your group will not be lecturing. Instead, she or he will be asking the questions found in this guide and encouraging the members of the group to discuss what they have learned.

3. Stick to the topic being discussed. These studies focus on a particular passage of Scripture. Only rarely should you refer to other portions of the Bible or outside sources. This allows for everyone to participate on equal ground and for in-depth study.

4. Be sensitive to the other members of the group. Listen attentively when they describe what they have learned. You may be surprised by their insights! Each question assumes a variety of answers. Many questions do not have "right" answers, particularly questions that aim at meaning or application. Instead the questions push us to explore the passage more thoroughly.

   When possible, link what you say to the comments of others. Also, be affirming whenever you can. This will encourage some of the more hesitant members of the group to participate.

5. Be careful not to dominate the discussion. We are sometimes so eager to express our thoughts that we leave too little opportunity for others to respond. By all means participate! But allow others to also.

6. Expect God to teach you through the passage being discussed and through the other members of the group. Pray that you will have an enjoyable and profitable time together, but also that as a result of the study you will find ways that you can take action individually and/ or as a group.

7. It will be helpful for groups to follow a few basic guidelines. These guidelines, which you may wish to adapt to your situation, should be read at the beginning of the first session.

   • Anything said in the group is considered confidential and will not be discussed outside the group unless specific permission is given to do so.

   • We will provide time for each person present to talk if he or she feels comfortable doing so.

   • We will talk about ourselves and our own situations, avoiding conversation about other people.

   • We will listen attentively to each other.

   • We will be very cautious about giving advice.

Additional suggestions for the group leader can be found at the back of the guide.

A DIFFERENT GOSPEL?

Galatians 1

Imagine that you are in central south Turkey during the reign of the Roman emperor Claudius. Most in the town worship one or other of the local gods or goddesses, several of whom claim the loyalty of particular racial groups. Some have started to worship the emperor himself, and with him the power of Rome.

There is also a significant minority of Jews, with their own synagogue. They are threatened by the growing power of the imperial cult, on top of the usual pagan idolatry and wickedness. And into this town has come a funny little Jew called Paul. According to Paul, there is one God, the world's creator, and this one God has now unveiled his long-awaited plan for the world. The unveiling took place in a Jew called Jesus, whom Paul says is the Jewish Messiah, a kind of king-to-end-all-kings.

OPEN

How do you determine whether a teacher or preacher is trustworthy?

relationship

STUDY

1. *Read Galatians 1:1-9*. The word *apostle* means "one who is sent," and came to be a technical term in early Christianity for the original ones whom Jesus sent out after his resurrection. Paul's opponents had persuaded the Galatians that Paul was only a secondhand apostle, that he got his apostleship and his message from other early Christians, not from Jesus himself.

   What does Paul stress about his own apostleship?

   gospel not of human origin
   revealed by God - face to face experience

2. How had the Galatian church shocked Paul?

   Deserting Christ - turning to diff gospel
   retreat from freedom

3. Jews believed that when the Messiah came he would be Lord of all the world; so, Paul argues, the Messiah would have to have just one family. So although this family is the fulfillment of what God had promised to the Jews, because of Jesus you don't have to be a Jew to belong. Paul's opponents insisted that if Gentile believers wanted to be part of the real inner circle, they had to become Jews. The "good news" according to his opponents was that you're welcome into God's family if you follow the Law of Moses.

   What could be attractive to people about a "gospel" which involved becoming a member of a family that followed the Law of Moses?

   tradition
   nothing more to think about

4. For Paul the *gospel* isn't a system of salvation or a new way of being religious. It's the announcement that Jesus, the crucified Messiah, is exalted as Lord of the whole world; therefore he is calling into existence a single worldwide family.

What conflicts have you witnessed—and perhaps even been caught up in—between different groups of people in a church or Christian fellowship?

5. *Read Galatians 1:10-24.* What criticism had been lodged against Paul as suggested by verse 10?

   seeking approval for self
   gospel of human origin

6. How does Paul use his personal story to verify his apostleship?

   He place he went - unknown

7. What is the value of church leaders honestly telling the stories of their own spiritual journeys?

   they are real

God revealed his Son to Saul of Tarsus in order that Saul, an ultra-orthodox Jew, might tell the pagan nations that Israel's God loved them just as much as he loved Israel. Paul must have learned his sense of irony from God himself!

8. "Then, after three years" (v. 18) refers to the aftermath of the events of Galatians 1:17. Paul had gone away to Arabia (probably Sinai) and then returned to Damascus before going to Jerusalem.

   Paul then notes in verse 22 that the little messianic assemblies in Judea—on their way to being what we would call churches, but at the moment simply synagogues whose members had all become Christians—had never met him. But what they heard about him, as he was starting his missionary work, was not "some wretched fellow is preaching a watered-down, distorted version of the gospel" but rather "the man we heard of as a great persecutor is preaching the faith he once tried to destroy." An independent apostle but with the same message.

How did the Judean Christians affirm Paul's message?

glorified God

9. Paul was now preaching the faith that he had once tried to destroy (v. 23). What is the most remarkable and even unlikely conversion to Christ that you have seen?

10. What struggles between two churches or Christian groups have you seen or known of?

11. Based on Galatians 1, what would Paul tell us is the answer to these struggles? *stay w/ the gospel of Christ*

12. What do we learn of the gospel from Galatians 1 so far?

Christ gave himself for our sins
grace for all

PRAY

Pray for discernment, humility and a desire for unity with other Christians. Pray that you will extend God's grace to the people around you.

2

AGREEMENT AND
CONFRONTATION

Galatians 2:1-14

A good deal of the letter to the Galatians hinges on the fact that circumcision was the key issue, almost to the point of obsession, in the churches where Gentiles had become members, including of course the churches founded by Paul himself. It was all a question of identity, of knowing not only who you were yourself but who else belonged in your group, your tribe, your ethnic family. It didn't matter in the very early church, because all the first Christians were Jews, so all the males were circumcised anyway. But as soon as non-Jews heard the good news of Jesus, believed it and got baptized, the question of group identity-markers surfaced, and surfaced quite violently.

OPEN

What would you say are the identity markers of a Christian?

grace
love
peace

STUDY

1. *Read Galatians 2:1-14.* Fourteen years after his first visit Paul returned to Jerusalem. He didn't go there to learn the gospel since he already knew it. What then was the purpose of his visit (vv. 1-2)?

   had a revelation

2. What conflict did Paul encounter in Jerusalem (vv. 3-5)?

   circumcision / truth of the gospel

3. Verse 4 refers to *slavery.* What does that slavery consist of?

   the law – spiritual occasions, seasons, Sacrifices

4. What rules or behaviors do various people say are necessary today to be a true Christian? *?*

Circumcision wasn't just a matter of keeping part of the Law of Moses. It was this sign of membership in the covenant family of God, which some Jewish Christians (who Paul calls false family members) said was also essential to the gospel. Over the centuries circumcision had become *the* marker of Israel's racial identity. Paul will insist in the course of this letter, however, that one does not need to become part of a certain race to join God's family.

5. The writing in verses 1-5 is jerky and difficult. Perhaps it reflects Paul's anger and frustration at the allegations against him. Yet Paul,

unlike some Christians today, did not dispute with his opponents for the sake of arguing, but "so that the truth of the gospel might be maintained for you" (v. 5). How can you or your church become known more for grace and truth?

6. What was the issue at stake in verses 6-10?

   grace given to Paul to share gospel w/ the Gentiles

7. How does Paul once again balance the case for his independent apostleship alongside the case for his unity with the rest of the church?

   he and Peter called to diff groups all together remember the poor

8. How did the leaders respond to what Paul told them?

   right hand of fellowship remember the poor

If Paul stressed too much the fact that James, Peter (also called Cephas) and John approved of his preaching the gospel to the Gentiles, his opponents would say "There you are! We told you! He just got it from them and now he's muddled it up, as we said!" But if he labored the point that God doesn't care who's who in the church, that all are equal in his sight and that the Jerusalem apostles are ultimately no more important than anyone else, he ran the risk of breaking fellowship with the center of Christian faith. For Paul the unity of the church was absolutely vital. Paul made it clear that he was not in the

pocket of the Jerusalem apostles. But he also made it clear that they
were very happy about him and his work.

9.   Paul and Barnabas went to Jerusalem from Antioch not only to meet
     with the apostles but to deliver an offering (Acts 11:27-30). They
     returned to Antioch; later Peter followed them there. What conflicts
     arose during Peter's time there (vv. 11-14)?

     Peter refusing to eat w/ gentiles

10. What is Paul referring to in verse 14 when he says they were out of
     line with gospel truth?

     hypocrisy

It's hard for Westerners today to see how serious a matter table fellowship was in the early church. If we are eating with colleagues
from work, we don't stop to inquire about their ethnic background.
A moment's thought, however, will remind us that there have been
and continue to be places in the world where if your skin is the wrong
color, or if you are known to belong to the wrong religion, or perhaps
simply if your accent gives you away as the wrong sort of person,
there will be some who will not sit down and eat with you. Eating
with people is one of the most powerful symbols of association.

11. Why would this story of Paul's confrontation with Peter be important
     to the church in Galatia—the recipients of this letter from Paul?

The real Peter is the Peter who knows in his bones that, in Jesus the

Messiah, God has created one new family of Jews and Gentiles. It's hard to live like that after a lifetime of looking at Gentiles as almost a different species; but Peter has been doing it. When hard-liners arrive who wouldn't approve of the Antioch practice, Peter holds the mask of Jewish respectability in front of his real face, which means that for the moment he will separate himself from the Gentile Christians. So convincing is his mask that the other Jewish Christians are taken in by it, even Barnabas.

12. Paul's confrontation with Peter wasn't just a squabble between two ways of interpreting one comparatively trivial point; it involved the very heart of the gospel. How do you discern the issues which really matter to the gospel?

PRAY

Confess any ways in which you separate yourself from other Christians in order to protect your own reputation. Forgive anyone who has done the same to you. Ask God to give you a more open heart toward believers who are different from you.

NOTE ON GALATIANS 2:14

What does Paul mean when he accuses Peter of living like a pagan or a Gentile? That Peter is eating pork or other forbidden food? Possible, but pretty unlikely. That Peter is disobeying the moral laws in Torah? Certainly not—Paul would have had other sharp words for that, as indicated in Galatians 5. That Peter is no longer saying his prayers? Highly unlikely.

Far and away the most likely solution is that Peter is no longer observing standard Jewish taboos. Peter was likely by now well and truly used to eating with Gentile Christians, and to making no difference between himself and them. That, after all, is what Acts says Peter had learnt in the house of Cornelius (Acts 10:28; 11:9). Paul is pointing out that Peter is acting like a hypocrite, deceitfully acting a part that he doesn't actually believe in. First Peter ate with non-Jewish people (which Paul says the gospel makes possible) and then Peter refused to do so for fear of what the circumcision group would think (which Paul condemns).

As we proceed to verse 16, the force of Paul's statement that we are not justified by works of the Mosaic Law is this: "Yes, you are Jewish; but as a Christian Jew you ought not to be separating on ethnic lines." In the immediate context Paul is saying that to be justified means, "to be reckoned by God to be a true member of his family, and hence with the right to share table fellowship." For Paul, "justification," whatever else it included, always had in mind God's declaration of membership, and that this always referred specifically to the coming together of Jews and Gentiles in faithful membership of the Christian family. (See my book *Justification: God's Plan and Paul's Vision*, chapter 5, for further comment on this passage.)

A NEW IDENTITY

Galatians 2:15–3:9

Beginning again from scratch to *learn who you are* is a strange idea for most of us. It is precisely what people who have suffered severe memory loss need to do. It is what people who have suffered other kinds of loss also need to do: the refugee without home, country or family is only one example. Precisely this sort of exercise, losing one identity and reconstructing another, is what Paul is explaining in this dense and complex passage. It isn't a matter of a few twists and turns in the interpretation of the gospel or the Jewish Law. It isn't about one style of missionary policy as against another. It is a matter of *who you are in the Messiah.*

OPEN

If someone asked you, "Who are you?" how would you answer? Would you answer differently depending on who asked you?

STUDY

1. *Read Galatians 2:15-21.* Often Paul's dense passages like this one

yield their secrets if you approach them from near the end, where
he sums up everything in a single great climactic statement. What
main points does he make in verses 19-20 about the true identity of
Christians? *died to the law*
living by faith in the Son of God
Christ lives in me ~loved me ~gave himself for me

2. My translation of verse 2:20 is, "And the life I do still live in the flesh,
I live within the faithfulness of the son of God, who loved me and gave
himself for me." How does this verse speak to the issue of whether
only Jewish Christians belong to the true people of God or whether in
Christ non-Jews can also belong without first becoming Jews?
faith in the Son of God all that matters

One of Paul's most well-known ideas remains difficult for modern
Western minds to come to terms with. Those who belong to the
Messiah (*Christ* in Greek) are *in the Messiah,* so that what is true
of him is true of them. The roots of this idea are in the Jewish be-
liefs that the king represents his people, as David represented Israel
against the Philistines when he fought Goliath. What is true of the
king is true of them.

3. How does Paul suggest in verse 2:19 that even as a Jew he deci-
sively left his Jewish identity behind by taking on his new identity
in Christ? *Through the law - died to the law*
what is our life in ~ our hope in?
our joy in?

4. Now we can go back to 2:15-16. *Justified* or *justification* means "being
declared righteous." Consider this translation of the Greek text in
verse 16:

But we know that a person is not declared "righteous" by works of the Jewish Law, but through the faithfulness of Jesus the Messiah.

That is why we too believed in the Messiah, Jesus: so that we might be declared "righteous" on the basis of the Messiah's faithfulness, and not on the basis of works of the Jewish Law. On that basis, you see, no creature will be declared "righteous."

What is the foundation of our being declared "righteous"?

Christ died for our sin

5. The heart of Paul's argument is that one must lose everything, including the memory of who one was before, and one must accept and learn to live by a new identity with a new foundation. What old identities have you discarded or should you discard because of being in Christ?

Paul's head-on clash with Peter in Antioch (2:11-14) was about Christian identity. His passionate appeal to the Galatians is about their Christian identity. The question Paul and Peter have run into, which was focused on whether Jewish and Gentile Christians were allowed to eat at the same table, is the question "Who is God's true Israel? Who are the true people of God?" Paul's answer is simple: all who are "in the Messiah" are the true people of God. That means believing Gentiles as well as believing Jews.

6. How does 2:17-18 reinforce the point Paul made to Peter?

Cant backtrack & include the law in the gospel

7. *Read Galatians 3:1-9.* What is Paul's reaction to the news that his beloved Galatians are thinking of getting circumcised and trying to

become part of the physical family of Israel (3:1-4)?

horrified

8. How does Paul make the case for the primacy of faith over the Jewish Law (3:5)? *God supplied the Spirit – not so you can live by the law, but by the Spirit*

9. Paul lines up "Spirit" and "faith" on the one hand, and "flesh" and "law" on the other. Why do you think human beings are so prone to fall back onto the flesh and law even after beginning with the Spirit and faith (3:3)?

It's easier

10. How is it that the Galatians are already children of Abraham without being circumcised (3:6-9)?

It was declared to Abraham

11. How does Paul further make his case in verses 3:8-9 that national or ethnic identity with Israel is not necessary?

Genesis 12 promises that God will bless all the nations through Abraham. Genesis 15 describes the covenant God made with Abraham, promising him a great family and the land as its inheritance. The critical move was that when God made the first promise, Abraham believed it. That doesn't mean his faith *earned* him his membership in God's covenant; the promise was already made. It was rather the badge that showed he was now in covenant with God.

12. How is your everyday life different because your identity is in Christ rather than in being part of a particular group?

PRAY

Thank God for the covenant status we have through Christ. Ask the Holy Spirit to prompt you back to Christ when you are tempted to rely on anything or anyone else.

NOTE ON GALATIANS 2:17-18

Paul is demonstrating to Peter that even Jewish Christians have lost their old identity, defined by the Law of Moses, and have come into a new identity, defined only by the Messiah. This doesn't mean, as he says in verses 17-18, that by losing Jewish identity we are "sinners," as the Jews had regarded the Gentiles. On the contrary, if like Peter you reconstruct the wall between Jews and Gentiles, all you achieve is to prove that you yourself are a lawbreaker. If the Jewish Law is what really matters, then look out: you've broken it!

But the Jewish Law isn't now the thing that matters. "If righteousness (covenant membership, in other words, justification) came by the Jewish Law, then the Messiah wouldn't have needed to die." To have separate tables within the church is to spurn the generous love of the Messiah. One of the marks of Jesus' public career was open table-fellowship. God intends it to be a mark of Jesus' people from that day to this.

A PROMISE FULFILLED

Galatians 3:10-22

God's promise to Abraham wasn't simply about the Jews; it was designed for all the nations. Abraham's family was to bring God's plan of salvation to the rest of the world. That's why there was such a family in the first place. But what had happened to this family? And what, in consequence, had happened to God's plan and purpose? The physical family of Abraham, the Jewish people, had overturned like a huge truck in the road and were now blocking the original intention. God's promise still held good; God still intended to bless the whole world through Abraham's family; but Israel, the promise bearers, were not only themselves failing, but getting in the way of the wider fulfillment.

OPEN

When have you especially benefited from someone keeping a promise?

STUDY

1. *Read Galatians 3:10-22.* How does Paul contrast the Law of Moses and faith?

   righteous live by faith, not the law

2. Why are those who try to live by Mosaic Law doomed from the start (vv. 10-11)?   *not possible*

3. What was the Messiah's way of redeeming his people (vv. 13-14)?

   becoming the ransom for us

4. How do you react to the statement that Christ himself became "a curse on our behalf" (v. 13)?

   took our sin on himself

We should look back to Galatians 3:7-9 to answer, What is the problem to which the curse-bearing death of the Messiah is the answer? The problem is that the Mosaic Law looked as if it would prevent the Abrahamic promises of blessing from getting out to the nations, and thus prevent the plan God always had for blessing the nations through Israel from coming to pass.

In short, the Law pronounced a curse on all who failed to keep it, so that Israel could not fulfill God's purpose. Instead, Paul insists, the Messiah has taken that curse upon himself, as Israel's representative. Jesus took the weight of Israel's curse on himself, not just in some abstract theological sense but quite literally and historically, when he died on the cross. The roadblock has been taken out of the way. The traffic can flow as God always intended it: from the promise of Abraham, through his family, his "seed" (in the person of Israel's representative, the Messiah) and out to the all the nations. Because of him, both Jews and Gentiles are offered full membership in his family.

5. How does Paul say can we be sure that the covenant with Abraham
   takes precedence over the Law of Moses (vv. 15-18)?

   the original promise

6. The next logical question is "Why then the Mosaic Law?" Paul asks
   the question himself. How does he answer it (vv. 19-22)?

   a temporary role – to deal w/ Transgressions

7. What is the relationship between the Law of Moses and promise (vv.
   21-22)?

   *not opposed to the promise)
   but never intended to give life*

The Mosaic Law was a necessary part of the intervening story between the giving of the promise and its fulfillment. Paul is quite
clear that the human race as a whole is sinful, under God's judg-
ment. He is also clear that God called Abraham so that eventually,
through his family, the remedy might be found for the problem of
human beings and indeed the cosmos as a whole. But Abraham's
family was also part of the human race. The people who carried the
solution were themselves part of the problem. The Mosaic Law was
given because of the in-between state of Abraham's physical family,
the people of Israel. It was given for a set period of time until the
single family intended and promised by God (of both Jew and Gentile) should arrive with the Messiah.

8. What does this passage have to teach us about the security of all
   who believe the gospel regardless of race or ethnic identity?

9. In verse 22 many Bible translations, instead of saying "faith in Jesus Christ," have "the faithfulness of Jesus Christ"—which makes more sense and is less redundant. How did Jesus prove himself faithful?

10. How has Jesus the Messiah proved himself faithful to you?

PRAY

Thank God for his promises and for the assurance that he keeps his promises. Thank Jesus the Messiah for the amazing magnitude of his love, even to becoming a curse for us.

NOTE ON GALATIANS 3:19-20

The Mosaic Law was given through the agency not only of angels (that is, for Paul, a way of saying that the Law was indeed God's Law, wonderful and holy) but also of the "mediator," that is, Moses. Moses, though, cannot be the mediator through whom God creates the "one," the single family he always wanted; but God is one, and so (as Paul explains in Romans 3:29-30) he desires a single family, not many families. Left to itself, the Law, putting Israel in quarantine as it did, would have created at least two families (Israel and believing Gentiles) and possibly many more.

THE COMING OF FAITH

Galatians 3:23–4:7

One of the worst evenings of my daughter's young life was when she was asked to be a babysitter for some friends—a job she had often done before, happily and successfully. Unknown to them or us, the two young children were in a very cross mood, and resented their parents going out for the evening. They took out their sulks and anger on my daughter. She had a miserable time, but managed to prevent the children doing anything too drastically wicked. She—and, I think, the children—were extremely relieved when the evening was over.

Paul pictures the Mosaic Law in the role of a babysitter until Israel should grow up. So Paul now asks the Galatians, do you want to go back to being a child, when you could be grown up? Do you want to go back to being a slave, when you could be free?

OPEN

Can you remember when you first realized you did not need to have a babysitter or someone to look after you at all times? If you have older children, when did you first realize that they did not need a sitter? What kind of feelings did those experiences cause?

STUDY

1. *Read Galatians 3:23-29*. Paul's basic point is about the story of Israel between the time of Moses and the coming of the Messiah. What was Israel's condition during that time (3:23-24)?

   imprisoned by the law
   guarded under the law

2. How have both Jew and Gentile become part of God's family (3:25-27)?

   all baptized into ~~the~~ Christ
   heirs thru Abraham

The word translated "guardian," "disciplinarian" or "babysitter" in verses 24-25 would normally, in Paul's world, refer to a slave whose task it was to look after the children day by day on the parents' behalf, taking them to school, making sure they were safe, keeping them out of mischief and so on. Many cultures still have people who fulfill such functions, who sometimes become honored members of the family after their child-related duties come to an end. The fact that Israel needed a babysitter during the period of childhood did not mean that the babysitter should continue to do the job once the child had grown up.

Paul is claiming throughout the letter that, with the coming of the Messiah, Israel was at last God's grown-up child. The badge of the grown-up child of God, the badge of God's free people, is that he trusts them with responsibility. They are people of faith, of trust. They believe the gospel.

3. How does Paul express the unity which Christ has brought about among believers (3:26-29)?

   all are children of God thru faith in Christ

4. What matters to Paul is that someone is in the Messiah or *belongs to* the Messiah. This is not merely a spiritual state resulting from or consisting in a certain type of inner experience. For Paul it is a matter of belonging to a particular community, the new royal family, the Messiah's people; and this family is entered through baptism. Paul knew that some people were slaves and others free. But the point is that *all these are irrelevant for your status in the family of the Messiah.* There aren't two families, one more privileged than the other. There is only one.

What ethnic, social and gender divisions still plague the church? *??*

5. How, in light of this passage, can we overcome these divisions?

acceptance of all in Christ

Theme of importance in inheritance

6. *Read Galatians 4:1-7.* Though in verse 3 Paul is talking about Jews ("we"), what he says about these Jews who have become Christians is designed to make their story as alike as possible to that of Gentile Christians. How were Jews and Gentiles both enslaved, according to Paul?

Jews to law
Gentiles w/out law
all designed to receive promise of Abraham (Christ) but enslaved because Christ not yet appeared

7. What changes have been brought about by both Jews' and Gentiles' adoption into God's family?

received Spirit
now child of God
an heir

Abraham's singular offspring Gen 12

These verses are full of the language of Exodus. God called Moses to lead Israel out of slavery in Egypt into freedom to inherit the Promised Land. Freedom was secured through Passover with the sacrifice of the lambs and the slaying of Egypt's firstborn. Then, when the people had left Egypt, they came to Sinai forty days after Passover, and they were given the Law by Moses as their guide through the wilderness to their inheritance. But then comes the new Passover. God sent out, not Moses, but his own Son, Jesus the Messiah, so that through his death freedom could be bought and the slaves could become true children. Forty days after Passover, on the feast of Pentecost, God gave, not the Law, but his own Spirit, the spirit of his Son, to turn his people into his true children in their innermost beings as well as in legal status. *gift of Spirit proves they are heirs*

8. How do you see the Trinity at work in these verses?

   God – Son – Spirit

9. In the Greek of verse 4:7 Paul suddenly shifts from the plural *you* to the singular *you*, pointing a finger at the reader. When did you first realize that the message of deliverance is not only for people in general but for you personally?

10. What are some situations in which you especially need to hear again that *you* as an individual are a child of God?

   Abraham justified by faith – all people of faith descendants

11. Where and how do you need to stand up and live like a child of
    God?

PRAY

The familiar name *Abba* or *Daddy* (4:6) was used by adult Jewish children as well as young ones; the point is not the age of the child but the
intimacy and familiarity of the word. Pray to your Father, thanking him
for the faithfulness of Christ and the freedom Christ has won for you.

No Turning Back

Galatians 4:8-20

The Galatian Christians have come out of the "Egypt" of idolatry, of worshiping false gods. They have been set free, redeemed by the personal action of the one true God in his Son and his Spirit (Galatians 4:4-7). Now it seems they have had a look at the wide and worrying world of freedom, and they don't like what they see. They are determined to return once more to the world where life seems safer, more regulated, where you know where you are: in other words, to the life of slavery. They are, Paul declares, choosing to go back where they were before, back to the old pagan gods they had worshiped until the time when they were set free by the living God.

OPEN

What do you sometimes wish you could go back to, physically or spiritually, because it seems safer?

The challenge

STUDY

1. *Read Galatians 4:8-11.* What causes Paul such amazement?

    want to be enslaved

2. How does Paul contrast the previous and the current state of the Galatians?

    didn't know God / now know God
    slaves / free

3. Why do you think Paul corrects himself from "you've come to know God" to "to be known *by* God" (v. 9)?

    must not know truly if you're
    turning back —

The Galatians are insisting on keeping the Jewish festivals (v. 10). Those festivals all looked forward to the great act of redemption which God would one day accomplish. So how can the Galatians keep the festivals when God's future has already arrived in Jesus Christ? By these observances they are saying that they aren't sure if God really has done what he said he would, whereas the whole point of the gospel is that he has!

4. Think of a time when you felt, like Paul, that your investment of time and energy in another person or cause might be wasted (v. 11). What led you to invest so much?

5. Even when it looked like your time and energy might turn out to be wasted, what gave you hope?

It's easier to rule your life by the old line-up of options: racial or tribal identity, geographical or territorial loyalty, the demands of money, sex and power. It's much harder to follow the God revealed in Jesus and the Spirit and to learn true freedom, true humanness, in the fellowship of other followers. But, as Paul will go on to say, there is no alternative. God has acted; we have tasted the effect of that action. If we go back now, we are denying not only ourselves and our Christian experience, but God himself.

now we know

6. *Read Galatians 4:12-20.* How and why does Paul change his tone?

*sympathetic
they was good to him*

7. How does Paul describe their relationship when he first came to the Galatians?

phys infirmity but welcomed - loved

8. Why does an appeal such as the one Paul makes here sometimes get through when a logical argument doesn't?

*relational
we're in this together*

9. The other group (v. 17), the circumcision party, wants to set up a two-level fellowship, an outer circle for Gentile Christians and an inner circle for Jewish Christians. But Paul knows that there can be no outer circle and inner circle within the grace of God. What is the appeal of an "inner circle"?

feel special — we're the 1st of Gods people

10. When have you seen Christians drawn in, and perhaps been drawn in yourself, by the promise of special status in an "inner circle"?

11. How does Paul use the surprising metaphor of childbirth for himself (v. 19)? *Start over again — re-birth them*

12. What does it mean for Christ to be formed in us? Give some practical examples.

*growing in fruits of the Spirit
Colossians 3:1-17*

PRAY

Paul shows the Galatians that he is not just a brain with a mouth attached, but a warm-hearted human being with a primary claim on their love and loyalty. Pray that in all your conversations about the gospel you will have a warm heart and genuine concern for the other person. Consider relationships in which you tend to use only intellectual argument, and ask God to fill you with compassion as well. Ask God to forgive you when you have supported an inner circle that kept others out.

NOTE ON GALATIANS 4:10

From very early on the Christian church kept various festivals: Paul himself speaks of the first day of the week as special (1 Corinthians 16:2), the day that had been made special forever by Jesus' resurrection. Likewise, Easter quickly became an important annual festival. So it can't be that all observances of days and times was to be banned. In any case, Paul himself says in Romans 14:5-6 that observing days or not observing them is something for individual Christians to decide as a matter of their own personal discipleship. The issue for Paul is also not that the Galatians might start to worship their old pagan deities, but that they want to become Jews. Circumcision was one evidence of that (Galatians 2:3, 12) and not eating with Gentiles was another (Galatians 2:12-14). Here is a third.

FREEDOM IN CHRIST

Galatians 4:21–5:6

Paul now offers a new picture to make his case about freedom in Christ. Back he goes to one of the least happy episodes in Genesis (16 and 21): the story of Abraham's wife, Sarah, and Abraham's concubine, Hagar, and their sons. God had promised Abraham a son (Genesis 15), but rather than wait Sarah suggested that, according to the customs of the time, he should have a child through her slave girl, Hagar. Abraham agreed, and Hagar gave birth to Ishmael.

Afterward Sarah too became pregnant and gave birth to Isaac. Some time later Sarah became jealous of Ishmael, because of her son Isaac, and dismissed him and his mother. Ishmael became the father of the peoples of Arabia: Isaac became the father of the people of Israel.

It is possible that Paul's opponents had been using the story of Abraham, Hagar and Sarah to reinforce their point that, though the Galatians might have come into God's people through believing the gospel, it looked as if there were now two families, both claiming to be Abraham's children. If that was so, they may have said, then the Jewish Christians must be the true free children, the descendants of Isaac; Gentile Christians, still uncircumcised, must be the children of Ishmael, the outsiders, the foreigners.

OPEN

When have you felt the most free, and why?

STUDY

1. *Read Galatians 4:21-31.* Who does Paul say Hagar, Sarah and their sons represent? *Hagar - slave - adopt gospel based on (Ishmael) Law (advocated by missionaries) Sarah - wife - Colatians - adopt Paul (Isaac) circumcision - free gospel*

2. Physically, the people promoting circumcision are Jews and are descendants of Isaac. How does Paul turn their argument on its head and say they are really descendants of Ishmael?

   going back to Law

3. Paul's opponents claim authority from Jerusalem. Who or what does Paul say are the two Jerusalems (4:25-26)?

   Hagar - Mt. Sinai - Arabia - present Jerusalem - law
   Sarah - the Jerusalem above - free

4. Paul makes the remarkable statement in verse 28 that the Galatians, who are Gentiles rather than Jews, are children of promise in the line of Isaac. How is this so?

   free of the Law

5. Have you ever looked on certain groups or types of Christian believers as not quite measuring up?

6. Why have you felt that way about them?

7. *Read Galatians 5:1-6.* Paul says in verse 1 that it is for freedom that we were set free. What does he mean by this?

    freedom in Christ free from law - but following

8. What *either-or* choice does Paul then put before the Galatian Christians? *The Law or Christ*

9. How does that *either-or* choice strike you?

If you get circumcised, Paul says, you are committing yourself to keeping the whole Law, the entire Jewish Torah. It isn't just a minor ritual requirement which can go comfortably alongside commitment to the Messiah. That is what the "agitators" have implied. But the only point of getting circumcised is if you are then intending to submit, in every other way as well, to the full discipline of the Jewish synagogue. For Paul the choice is absolute.

10. Instead of the Mosaic Law indicating whether we are part of God's family, what does Paul say in 5:5-6 are the true marks that we belong?

righteousness
faith working thru love

11. How is faith showing itself through love (5:6) different from following laws about circumcision or eating?

requires being "in Christ"

12. How can your faith work through love this week?

PRAY

Praise God for your freedom in Christ. Pray that he will show you any ways in which you are still in bondage to the Mosaic Law, and show you how to live by love in faith.

NOTE ON GALATIANS 5:4

Being "alienated" or "severed" or "cut off" from the Messiah is not merely a theological category. It is something you can see going on when you sit down and eat. Here are the Messiah's family, this motley crew, eating together: Peter, Paul and Barnabas, mixed up with Gentile Christians in Antioch; the Galatian Christians, mostly ex-pagans, prior to the arrival of the "agitators." This is the Messiah's family. And if you separate yourself from this family, you separate yourself from the Messiah. That's what's going on.

3∴ 4   3∴ 11

NOTE ON GALATIANS 5:5

The *hope* of righteousness? Has Paul not declared in chapters 2 and 3 that
those who believe in the Messiah already have "righteousness," already
hear the verdict in their favor, "you are my children, my justified ones"?
Yes, but Paul has not forgotten that this remains a future reality, inau-
gurated indeed in the Messiah but awaiting its full consummation, and
that there is still to come a moment when the secrets of all hearts will be
revealed, when the verdict issued in the present will be reaffirmed at last.
And the proper stance of the Christian in this interim period, this now-
and-not-yet time, remains one characterized by three things: the Spirit,
faith and patient waiting. (See my book *Justification: God's Plan and Paul's
Vision*, chapter 5, for further comment on Galatians 5.)

SPIRIT AND FLESH

Galatians 5:7-21

For Paul the Galatian controversy isn't a matter of people choosing one religious option or another, finding a way forward on a spiritual journey; it's a matter of truth. If it is true that the Messiah has died and been raised (and if that isn't true Paul knows he would be wasting his time and his life), then this in turn establishes a network of truth that carries its own persuasive power. The Galatians, however, have been persuaded for the moment by some "agitator" not to believe it (Galatians 5:7, 10). If the Galatians give in on this one thing, circumcision, they won't simply be all right in everything else, with one little blemish. Their mistake will be like leaven in dough, and it will change everything.

why?

OPEN

When you hear yourself quoted as saying something you didn't really say, how do you react? How do you feel about it? How do you deal with it?

STUDY

1. *Read Galatians 5:7-12.* What harm had been done to the Galatians by
   an unnamed person or group?

   *distracted them from following Christ —
   running the race*

2. How does Paul encourage the Galatians (5:7, 10)?

   *7 you were running well
   10 confident in your thought process*

3. How does Paul suggest he was being misrepresented (5:11)?

   *if he was preaching circumcision,
   he wouldn't he still persecuted*

4. What does Paul mean in verse 11 when he says the cross is an of-
   fense or scandal (the word *scandal* means "something people trip
   over")?

   *if preached circumcision, no
   cross, no scandal —
   wouldn't be persecuted*

5. Does the cross offend people in the same way today? Explain.

6. Why do you think Paul expressed such extreme views as in verse
   12?

   he's all about it — fed up

Church people and theologians can become so affable, so friendly, so nice to everybody that we fail to confront head-on false teachings that can do lasting damage to churches and individual Christians. Maybe the only way we can get our message through is by vivid language, multiple imagery, not just keeping people awake but shocking them into seeing what the real issues are.

7. *Read Galatians 5:13-21.* Freedom *from* restraint, if it is to be of any use, must be matched by a sense of freedom *for* a particular purpose. What is God's purpose in our freedom in Christ (5:13-14)?

to live in Christ - in love - follow - love your neighbor

8. Why and how (according to Paul) is strife among Christians so destructive? *destroys the gospel*

As so often in Paul, *flesh* and *spirit* are in opposition to each other. This isn't a matter of the material world against the non-material. A wicked disembodied spirit could practice many of the works of the flesh. It is rather a matter of where your true identity lies, where your deepest motivation comes from and where the power that rules your life is found.

9. What are some practical ways you can show love toward those you have conflict with? *particular*

do not be angry - respond w/ kindness listen - respect other opinions

10. What have been some personal examples for you of verse 5:16 in action?

11. Paul mentions over a dozen different works of the flesh. What three or four different groups would you categorize these into, and why?

sexual
, idols
disagreement
disrespect for body

12. The *works of the flesh* (5:19-21) all sound quite worldly. How do you account for the fact that these sins also occur among Christians?

humans struggle
don't stay attached to Jesus

13. What do you find most encouraging in this passage?
the Spirit can lead us ; guide us,
enable us
V: 16

PRAY

Pray that you and other members of your Christian fellowship will become each other's servants, through love (5:13). Pray that the Holy Spirit will take that idea out of the abstract and show you specific ways to live it out.

What is your nickname and how did you get it?

9

FRUIT OF THE SPIRIT

Galatians 5:22–6:5

If Paul is famous for his contrast of *flesh* and *spirit*, he is also famous for the key words he uses that go with them both. He speaks of the *works of the flesh*, but the *fruit* of the Spirit. Compare artificial Christmas trees with ordinary but real fruit trees in an orchard. The Christmas trees look wonderful for a short while, but then they get packed away or thrown out. The fruit trees may not look so spectacular, but if they are properly cared for they will go on bearing fruit year after year. Which is more important? You hardly have to ask.

OPEN

How do you know if someone's faith in Christ is genuine?

Know them by their fruits

STUDY

1. *Read Galatians 5:22-26.* "But" is in contrast to the works of the flesh in 5:19-21. Consider the qualities in verses 22-23 one at a time. Who comes to mind when you think of each fruit of the Spirit?

2. Often when people emphasize the need for love, patience, gentleness and the like, this goes with an attitude to truth and the gospel which says that we shouldn't stress the things we disagree on. Equally, when people are passionate for the truth of the gospel, they often allow that zeal to betray them into the kind of anger and even malice that are listed under the works of the flesh.

In specific ways, how can we balance love with our passion for truth?

3. What are the implications of our being crucified with Christ (5:24)?

our passions and desires

4. How are we to cooperate with the Spirit (5:25)?

be guided

5. In what areas of life can you more fully line up with the Spirit?

most impt. thing

5

The nine qualities in verses 22-23 are not things which, if we try hard enough, we could simply do without help, without the Spirit. The point of all of them is that when the Spirit is at work they will begin to happen; new motivations will appear. When these qualities appear, with all their quiet joy, all their rich contribution to the sort of community God intends and will eventually produce, they come like the fruit in an orchard, not like the baubles on a Christmas tree. They will truly be part of who we will have become. Equally, as Paul shows by putting "self-control" at the end of the list, the way we become this kind of person is through Spirit-led hard moral choices.

6. Paul has just sketched out what life should be like if people are lining up with the Spirit. Now he applies this to the church's inner life. *Read Galatians 6:1-5.* What attitudes are Christians to have toward each other? *Spirit of gentleness*
bear one anothers burdens
watch out for pride
carry your own load - test yourself

7. Have you ever been called on to set someone right, and has anyone ever done the same for you (6:1)? How did the approach measure up to verse 1? *spirit of gentleness*

8. Why do you think Paul uses the word *law* in verse 6:2? *They know about "law" & has been explaining the law of Christ is love love fulfills the law*

9. Who has helped carry your burdens and how (6:2)?
think they are "something"

10. In Galatia people saw themselves as one particular type of Christian and looked down on the other types (6:3). If they saw one of the others doing something wrong, they would feel smug; that, they would think, is not the way "we" behave. At the same time, these groups were defined in terms of status, not detailed behavior; "we" (the Jewish Christians among them or the richer Christians or the ones who were also Roman citizens?) were simply different because they were different. Instead of the community Paul had established, where all were equal at the foot of the cross, all equally

"in Christ," all equally members of Abraham's family (3:26-29), the work of the agitators had left a legacy of division based on non-theological factors.

After encouraging humility in verse 6:3, Paul immediately says we can also have reason for pride in verse 6:4. How do these fit together?

no comparisons — no competing
v. 5 do what your called to do
no gifts better than others

11. How has Paul himself lived out 6:1-5?

always thinking of others

12. "Carry your own load" (6:5) would seem to contradict "carry each other's burdens" (6:2). How do you balance these two commands?

as to

PRAY

Pray that the Holy Spirit will display his fruit through you daily. Ask God to show you those whose burdens you need to help carry. Also ask him to show you where you have been shirking your responsibilities and need to start carrying your own load.

PRACTICAL WORDS
IN CLOSING

Galatians 6:6-18

It is difficult to ask people to give money, even for the best of causes. In this passage Paul manages to write about money without ever mentioning the word. Clearly the subject was as delicate in his world as it is in ours. Although the first part of this passage has wider applications, its central point is the quite specific one of financing the ministry and life of the church.

OPEN

If you had to give parting words to a group of people who are very dear to you, what would you say?

STUDY

1. *Read Galatians 6:6-10.* What are Paul's rationales for contributing to the work of the church?

reap what we sow
reap eternal life
our work should be for good of all - esp. family of faith

2. Why is money and church often such a sensitive topic?

3. General phrases like "do good to everybody" (v. 10) were in regular use in Paul's world, referring to financial contributions in civic and community life. How do Paul's images of reaping and sowing fit into this context?

growing the Kingdom

4. In verse 9 Paul warns against losing enthusiasm and becoming weary of right living. What has caused you to become weary and caused your enthusiasm to lag?

5. How have you been encouraged again?

The Christian view of money is that it is a responsibility given by God. It is never purely for one's own enjoyment; it is held in trust. If church members sow to the Spirit by giving solid practical support to the church's ministry, especially in teaching and preaching, they themselves will in due course bring in a harvest. If, however, they sow to the flesh, then all they will have to show for it will be the corruption and decay to which everything in the world is ultimately subject. The ministry of the word builds up people and communities. The life they then have will gloriously outlast death itself.

6. You know a letter is from a real, living, breathing human being when your correspondent takes the trouble not only to sign his or her name but also to add a few final sentences in personal handwriting. While Paul had been dictating this letter to a scribe, he now takes up his pen to write more than just his name. *Read Galatians 6:11-18.*

As Paul concludes his letter to the Galatian church, what is uppermost in his mind? *the circumcision issue*
all about Christ; a new creation is everything! no distinction before. Gentile & Jew

7. How might submitting to circumcision avoid persecution (vv. 12-13)? *sticking w/ Jewish law*

8. What do you think it means to "boast" in the cross of Jesus (v. 14)? *Christ is all there is - all That means anything to me*

9. Who is now God's true, fulfilled Israel (v. 16)? *all who believe as he does*

10. Paul writes that if it's bodily marks you want, it is the signs of the cross, not the circumciser's knife, that matter. The signs of the cross are the marks of persecution, the "wounds of Jesus" (v. 17). How have you been wounded for Christ, whether physically, emotionally, financially or in some other way?

11. What makes the wounds worth bearing?

    Christ alone is our salvation

12. The final lines of the letter are a benediction not only on the Galatians but on all of us who read these words. It is all of grace from start to finish: the grace of our Lord Jesus, the Messiah. The gospel does not come from human sources, and membership in the Messiah's people is not defined by human categories. Grace reaches out and embraces the whole world. The sign of that embrace is the presence and joy of the Spirit.

    Look back over this entire study of Galatians. How has your idea of God's grace in Christ been strengthened, challenged or confirmed?

PRAY

Taking verse 14 as your guide, pray that the world's ideas of achievement will be less and less important to you, and that the cross of Jesus will become more and more the central reality of your life. Thank God for his grace, and ask him to warn you when you start to depend on anything besides his grace.

GUIDELINES FOR LEADERS

My grace is sufficient for you.
(2 Corinthians 12:9)

If leading a small group is something new for you, don't worry. These sessions are designed to flow naturally and be led easily. You may even find that the studies seem to lead themselves!

This study guide is flexible. You can use it with a variety of groups—students, professionals, coworkers, friends, neighborhood or church groups. Each study takes forty-five to sixty minutes in a group setting.

You don't need to be an expert on the Bible or a trained teacher to lead a small group. These guides are designed to facilitate a group's discussion, not a leader's presentation. Guiding group members to discover together what the Bible has to say and to listen together for God's guidance will help them remember much more than a lecture would.

There are some important facts to know about group dynamics and encouraging discussion. The suggestions listed below should equip you to effectively and enjoyably fulfill your role as leader.

PREPARING FOR THE STUDY

1. Ask God to help you understand and apply the passage in your own life. Unless this happens, you will not be prepared to lead others. Pray too for the various members of the group. Ask God to open

your hearts to the message of his Word and motivate you to action.

2. Read the introduction to the entire guide to get an overview of the topics that will be explored.

3. As you begin each study, read and reread the assigned Bible passage to familiarize yourself with it. This study guide is based on the For Everyone series on the New Testament (published by SPCK and Westminster John Knox). It will help you and the group if you have on hand a copy of the companion volume from the For Everyone series both for the translation of the passage found there and for further insight into the passage.

4. Carefully work through each question in the study. Spend time in meditation and reflection as you consider how to respond.

5. Write your thoughts and responses in the space provided in the study guide. This will help you to express your understanding of the passage clearly.

6. It may help to have a Bible dictionary handy. Use it to look up any unfamiliar words, names or places. The glossary at the end of each New Testament for Everyone commentary may likewise be helpful for keeping discussion moving.

7. Reflect seriously on how you need to apply the Scripture to your life. Remember that the group members will follow your lead in responding to the studies. They will not go any deeper than you do.

LEADING THE STUDY

1. At the beginning of your first time together, explain that these studies are meant to be discussions, not lectures. Encourage the members of the group to participate. However, do not put pressure on those who may be hesitant to speak—especially during the first few sessions.

2. Be sure that everyone in your group has a study guide. Encourage the group to prepare beforehand for each discussion by reading the

introduction to the guide and by working through the questions in each study.

3. Begin each study on time. Open with prayer, asking God to help the group to understand and apply the passage.

4. Have a group member read aloud the introduction at the beginning of the discussion.

5. Discuss the "Open" question before the Bible passage is read. The "Open" question introduces the theme of the study and helps group members to begin to open up, and can reveal where our thoughts and feelings need to be transformed by Scripture. Reading the passage first will tend to color the honest reactions people would otherwise give—because they are, of course, supposed to think the way the Bible does. Encourage as many members as possible to respond to the "Open" question, and be ready to get the discussion going with your own response.

6. Have a group member read aloud the passage to be studied as indicated in the guide.

7. The study questions are designed to be read aloud just as they are written. You may, however, prefer to express them in your own words.

There may be times when it is appropriate to deviate from the study guide. For example, a question may have already been answered. If so, move on to the next question. Or someone may raise an important question not covered in the guide. Take time to discuss it, but try to keep the group from going off on tangents.

8. Avoid answering your own questions. An eager group quickly becomes passive and silent if members think the leader will do most of the talking. If necessary repeat or rephrase the question until it is clearly understood, or refer to the commentary woven into the guide to clarify the context or meaning.

9. Don't be afraid of silence in response to the discussion questions. People may need time to think about the question before formulating their answers.

10. Don't be content with just one answer. Ask, "What do the rest of you think?" or "Anything else?" until several people have given answers to the question.

11. Try to be affirming whenever possible. Affirm participation. Never reject an answer; if it is clearly off-base, ask, "Which verse led you to that conclusion?" or again, "What do the rest of you think?"

12. Don't expect every answer to be addressed to you, even though this will probably happen at first. As group members become more at ease, they will begin to truly interact with each other. This is one sign of healthy discussion.

13. Don't be afraid of controversy. It can be very stimulating. If you don't resolve an issue completely, don't be frustrated. Explain that the group will move on and God may enlighten all of you in later sessions.

14. Periodically summarize what the group has said about the passage. This helps to draw together the various ideas mentioned and gives continuity to the study. But don't preach.

15. Conclude your time together with the prayer suggestion at the end of the study, adapting it to your group's particular needs as appropriate. Ask for God's help in following through on the applications you've identified.

16. End on time.

Many more suggestions and helps for studying a passage or guiding discussion can be found in *How to Lead a LifeGuide Bible Study* and *The Big Book on Small Groups* (both from InterVarsity Press/USA).

Other InterVarsity Press Resources from N. T. Wright

The Challenge of Jesus: Rediscovering Who Jesus Was & Is
N. T. Wright offers clarity and a full accounting of the facts of the life and teachings of Jesus, revealing how the Son of God was also solidly planted in first-century Palestine. *978-0-8308-2200-3, 202 pages, hardcover*

Resurrection
This 50-minute DVD confronts the most startling claim of Christianity—that Jesus rose from the dead. Shot on location in Israel, Greece and England, N. T. Wright presents the political, historical and theological issues of Jesus' day and today regarding this claim. Wright brings clarity and insight to one of the most profound mysteries in human history. Study guide included. *978-0-8308-3435-8, DVD*

Evil and the Justice of God
N. T. Wright explores all aspects of evil and how it presents itself in society today. Fully grounded in the story of the Old and New Testaments, this presentation is provocative and hopeful; a fascinating analysis of and response to the fundamental question of evil and justice that faces believers. *978-0-8308-3398-6, 176 pages, hardcover*

Evil
Filmed in Israel, South Africa and England, this 50-minute DVD confronts some of the major "evil" issues of our time—from tsunamis to AIDS—and puts them under the biblical spotlight. N. T. Wright says there is a solution to the problem of evil, if only we have the honesty and courage to name it and understand it for what it is. Study guide included. *978-0-8308-3434-1, DVD*

Small Faith—Great God
N. T. Wright reminds us that what matters is not how much faith we have as who our faith is in. Wright looks at the character of the faith God calls us to. He unfolds how dependence, humility and mystery all have a role to play. But the author doesn't ignore the messiness and difficulties of life, when hard times come and the unexpected knocks us down. He opens to us what faith means in times of trial and even in the face of death. Through it all he reminds us, it's not great faith we need: it is faith in a great God. *978-0-8308-3833-2, 176 pages, hardcover*

Justification: God's Plan and Paul's Vision
In this comprehensive account and defense of the crucial doctrine of justification, Wright also responds to critics who have challenged what has come to be called the New Perspective. Ultimately, he provides a chance for those in the

middle of and on both sides of the debate to interact directly with his views and form their own conclusions. *978-0-8308-3863-9, 279 pages, hardcover*

Colossians and Philemon
In Colossians, Paul presents Christ as "the firstborn over all creation," and appeals to his readers to seek a maturity found only Christ. In Philemon, Paul appeals to a fellow believer to receive a runaway slave in love and forgiveness. In this volume N. T. Wright offers comment on both of these important books. *978-0-8308-4242-1, 199 pages, paperback*